AS/A-Level
Religious Studies

Philosophy

Philip Allan, an imprint of Hodder Education, an Hachette UK company, Market Place, Deddington, Oxfordshire OX15 0SE

Orders

Bookpoint Ltd, 130 Milton Park, Abingdon, Oxfordshire OX14 4SB
tel: 01235 827827   fax: 01235 400401   e-mail: education@bookpoint.co.uk

Lines are open 9.00 a.m.–5.00 p.m., Monday to Saturday, with a 24-hour message answering service. You can also order through our website: www.philipallan.co.uk

© Philip Allan Publishers 2010
ISBN 978-1-4441-0912-2

First published in 2004 as *Flashrevise Cards*

Impression number   5   4   3   2
Year   2015   2014   2013   2012

Printed in India

Hachette UK's policy is to use papers that are natural, renewable and recyclable products and made from wood grown in sustainable forests. The logging and manufacturing processes are expected to conform to the environmental regulations of the country of origin.

P01661

Plato

Q1 Who was Plato's famous teacher?

Q2 What was the name and purpose of the School he founded?

Q3 According to Plato, what was the only source of true knowledge?

Q4 Why can't objects in the physical world be the source of true knowledge?

ANSWERS

the teachings of Plato form the basis of much Western philosophy

A1 Socrates; he wrote nothing himself but was the subject of Plato's dialogues

A2 the Academy; its purpose was to train a new type of politician who would learn to be a philosopher ruler

A3 that which is permanent, unchanging, non-contingent and unseen; physical reality is a pale copy of true reality

A4 because physical things are constantly changing and are capable of decay

examiner's **note** Don't fall into the trap of thinking of Plato as a Christian — he lived long before Jesus was even born.

 **ANSWERS**

Plato's key ideas (1)

Q1 Give a brief outline of the allegory of the cave.

Q2 Why does Plato think that the allegory depicts the mind of an unthinking man?

Q3 What is the highest of the Forms?

Q4 How does humanity view the unchanging realities (Forms)?

ANSWERS

differences between the world of appearances and real world; ideas on unchanging goodness and reality

A1 a group of chained prisoners can only look ahead; a fire behind them throws shadows on the wall; the prisoners know nothing of life outside the cave, so they believe that the shadows are reflective of reality

A2 the unthinking man accepts what he sees and hears without question and has no awareness of Plato's realm of the Forms

A3 the absolute Form of the Good

A4 through the mind, soul or intellect

examiner's **note** Underlying these key ideas is Plato's belief that true knowledge comes from that which humanity has found out to be true after long and rigorous intellectual searching.

 **2 ANSWERS**

Plato's key ideas (2)

Q1 Why, according to Plato, did the Forms prove that humans have immortal souls?

Q2 What is anamnesis?

Q3 What does Plato mean by the pre-existent soul?

Q4 What happens to the soul after the physical body dies?

ANSWERS

since humans recognise the Form of the Good, they must have souls

A1 because humans instinctively recognise the Form of the Good, we must have encountered the Forms before we entered the physical world, thus proving we have immortal souls

A2 non-forgetting — the soul does not forget what it has encountered

A3 the soul that exists before it enters the physical body to live on earth

A4 the soul re-enters the eternal realm

examiner's **note** Platonic ideas on the afterlife are dualistic, reflecting his belief that the physical and non-physical are distinct. The physical invariably hinders the non-physical, since the needs of the physical (e.g. hunger, thirst and tiredness) intrude on the efforts made by the soul to contemplate the unseen, greater reality.

(**3**) **ANSWERS**

Aristotle

Q1 Who was Aristotle's famous teacher?

Q2 What School did Aristotle establish?

Q3 Aristotle was an empiricist philosopher. What does this mean?

Q4 Why did Aristotle reject Plato's theory of the Forms?

ANSWERS

Aristotle taught Alexander the Great

A1 Plato; Aristotle joined the Academy, attending Plato's lectures for 20 years

A2 the Lyceum; Aristotle was passed over as head of the Academy because of the divergence of his views from those of Plato

A3 he used sense experience to discover what he felt was the truth; he claimed that touch was the most rudimentary sense, hearing the most instructive and sight the most ennobling

A4 he believed that reality could be found in the physical world and that real substance was not found in the abstract, but in the concrete

***examiner's* note** Aristotle's philosophy was influential on the later development of classical arguments for the existence of God. He maintained that all things have a purpose, or *telos*, and that existence was dependent on a prime mover.

 **4 ANSWERS**

Aristotle and the principle of cause

Q1 What questions did Aristotle consider were answered by identifying the material and efficient causes of an item or being?

Q2 What questions were answered by identifying the formal and final causes?

Q3 What did Aristotle call God and what did he believe motivated God to act?

Q4 For what reason, did Aristotle believe, are all things drawn to God?

ANSWERS

Aristotle believed that the nature of everything was defined by its cause

A1 the questions 'What does it consist of?' and 'How did it happen?'; the material cause is the substance from which things are made and the efficient cause is the means by which things are created

A2 the questions 'What are its characteristics?' and 'Why is it here or what is its purpose?'; the formal cause is the design of an object and the final cause is its purpose or function

A3 the necessary first mover; he believed God was motivated by love

A4 because they seek to be in the image of God's perfection

***examiner's* note** Thomas Aquinas based part of his Cosmological Argument on the teachings of Aristotle.

5 ANSWERS

The God of classical theism

Q1 What is meant by 'omnipotent'?

Q2 What is meant by 'omniscient'?

Q3 What is meant by 'omni-benevolent?'

Q4 What does it mean to speak of God as eternal?

ANSWERS

A1 all powerful

A2 all knowing

A3 all loving/all good

A4 that God has no beginning or end

***examiner's* note** These attributes of God lead to many of the classical problems in the philosophy of religion, such as the problem of evil or questions about how far God is involved in the world.

Omnipotence and omniscience

Q1 What did Aquinas believe that an omnipotent God could not do?

Q2 What two powers of God did William of Ockham suggest that God possessed?

Q3 Why does God's omniscience pose problems for the existence of evil and suffering?

Q4 What does it mean to speak of God's knowledge being 'unearned'?

ANSWERS

A1 sin, since to sin was to fall short of a perfect action

A2 *potentia absoluta* — the power to do anything; *potentia ordinata* — God's choice to maintain a certain order until the end of time

A3 if God knows all, past, present and future, why does he not prevent occurrences of evil and suffering?

A4 God has not had to learn information in the way that humans have to

***examiner's* note** Aquinas observed that those things that God could not do were those things that could not be done because it would be logically impossible for them to be done.

(7) ANSWERS

God's goodness

Q1 What does it mean to say that God is the ground of moral values?

Q2 What does it mean to say that there is a tension between God's love and his wrath in the Bible?

Q3 What is grace?

Q4 What problem is presented to the conservative Christian by the notion of God's goodness?

ANSWERS ▶▶

A1 that humans cannot know what is good apart from God's revelation — God establishes what is morally good and makes it known to his people

A2 that God is called to punish those who are disobedient to him, but he does so reluctantly because he loves them (see Hosea 9:11)

A3 God's undeserved favour to humans

A4 the possibility that God will withhold punishment from those who have disobeyed him

***examiner's* note** God's goodness is ultimately expressed in the sending of Jesus to die on the cross: 'For God so loved the world, he gave his only Son, so all who believe in him should not perish but have eternal life' (John 3:16).

8 **ANSWERS**

God as creator (1)

Q1 How many accounts of creation can be found in Genesis?

Q2 What does creation *ex nihilo* mean?

Q3 What, according to the Bible, is the climax of God's creation?

Q4 What distinguishes humanity from the rest of creation?

ANSWERS ▶▶

A1 Two: Genesis 1, the Priestly account; and Genesis 2, the Jahwist account

A2 creation out of nothing

A3 humans — they are the final act of creation in Genesis 1, and the first in Genesis 2; they are given dominance and the responsibility of stewardship over the rest of creation, which is for their benefit

A4 human beings are made in the image of God

examiner's **note** Questions on this topic require an understanding of the nature of God, and the Bible is a rich source of material. Don't ignore it or confuse using it in an academic context with preaching.

9 **ANSWERS**

God as creator (2)

Q1 How did some early Christian thinking adapt the view of God as creator?

Q2 What is 'emanation'?

Q3 What biblical episode could be seen as the antithesis of the creation narrative?

Q4 Suggest an analogy that might help explain how God may have created *ex nihilo*.

ANSWERS

'God as creator' has been adapted within Christian thought over time, and continues to be redefined as science opens up new understandings

A1 some thinkers, such as Justin Martyr, suggested that God gave order to pre-existent matter, rather than creating *ex nihilo*

A2 the notion that the creation of the world was an overflowing of God's creative energy, showing his divine nature

A3 the Flood narrative (Genesis 6–8)

A4 as an artist creates out of nothing, so God creates the world as an expression of love

***examiner's* note** The biblical understanding of God as creator shares many similarities with other ancient traditions, such as the Babylonian epic *Emua Elish*.

(10) **ANSWERS**

God's revelation

Q1 What does it mean to say God is immanent?

Q2 What is the Euthyphro Dilemma?

Q3 What is the Decalogue more popularly known as?

Q4 What does it mean to say God is transcendent?

ANSWERS

A1 he can be known through experience and through the world

A2 does God create moral standards, or does he command what he already knows to be good?; this poses a significant problem for religious morality — if God does not create moral standards, where do they come from? If God does create morality, then anything he declares to be good is good by definition, e.g. even if he commanded humans to commit murder

A3 the Ten Commandments, found in Exodus 20:1–17

A4 God is beyond human experience and the world

***examiner's* note** The relationship of God to humanity is a crucial part of any question involving proof of the existence of God — in particular, religious faith depends on a personal experience of God.

(11) ANSWERS

Principles of philosophical proof

Q1 What, philosophically speaking, is a proof?

Q2 What is probability?

Q3 Why does the use of probability require us to make judgements?

Q4 What does 'logically necessary' mean?

ANSWERS ⟩⟩

A1 an argument that starts from one or more premises and argues to a conclusion

A2 the likelihood of an event occurring or of a claim being true

A3 we need to examine and evaluate the evidence and consider alternatives before making a judgement

A4 it applies to a set of premises and a conclusion that cannot be disputed, e.g. 'a circle is round'

examiner's **note** Good answers rely on the correct use of technical terms — and these are some of the most important. Make sure you understand them and can apply them in context.

Types of proof

Q1 What is an analytical or deductive proof?

Q2 What is an inductive or synthetic proof?

Q3 What is an *a priori* proof?

Q4 What is an *a posteriori* proof?

ANSWERS ⟩⟩

principles which must be understood before engaging in philosophical investigation

A1 a proof based on premises that are not drawn from experience, but that contain logically necessary conclusions, e.g. 'the queen is a woman'

A2 a proof based upon premises drawn from experience that do not contain logically necessary conclusions, e.g. 'the sun will shine in August'

A3 a proof in which we learn no more from the conclusion than we already knew from the premises, and which uses analytic terms that cannot be misinterpreted

A4 a proof which does not contain the conclusion within its premises; the more evidence stating factors we employ, the greater the likelihood of the conclusion being correct, but it can always be disproved

examiner's **note** Even if you are not asked directly about these concepts, you will need to use them in your answers on arguments for the existence of God.

(13) ANSWERS

Faith

21 What, philosophically speaking, is faith?

22 What is the propositional view of faith?

23 What is the non-propositional view of faith?

24 What is the difference between knowledge and faith?

ANSWERS ▶▶

for religious believers, faith is often the ultimate proof of the existence of God

A1 believing in something without proof; being certain of what you believe

A2 belief that there is an objective reality, which is called God

A3 belief that is not supported by empirical evidence or experience, but is based in some personal experience of God

A4 knowledge is based on a verifiable synthetic or analytic claim; faith is essentially non-verifiable

***examiner's* note** There is no single definition of faith. Make sure, in answering questions, that you state clearly what you mean by faith. One useful definition, found in the New Testament, is: 'Now faith is to be sure of what we hope for and certain of what we do not see' (Hebrews 11:1).

(14) ANSWERS

The Cosmological Argument

21 In which work did Aquinas outline his arguments concerning the existence of God?

22 Is the Cosmological Argument *a priori* or *a posteriori*, and why?

23 What is a contingent being?

24 What is a necessary being?

ANSWERS

explains the existence of the universe by reference to causes outside itself

A1 *Summa Theologica*; Aquinas proposed Five Ways that proved the existence of God

A2 *a posteriori*, because it assumes that the existence of the universe can be explained by reference to an external agent

A3 one which depends on other beings for its existence; it can also be called a possible being, e.g. humans, animals, the natural world

A4 a being that is not dependent on other beings for its existence; the Cosmological Argument depends on the notion that God is the necessary being who curtails the contingent universe

examiner's **note** The essence of the argument is that the universe is not self-explanatory and demands that we question its origin, nature and purpose.

 **15** **ANSWERS**

Aquinas' First Way

21 What did Aquinas define with the words 'the reduction of something from potentiality to actuality'?

22 What constitutes motion?

23 Why must there be a first mover?

24 What does *de re* mean?

ANSWERS

A1 motion

A2 a change of state in an item, being or state of affairs

A3 because things cannot move themselves

A4 it means 'concerning the thing itself' or 'in the nature of things'; if the universe is created by God then, if the universe exists, God must exist too — the nature of the universe demands that God exists

***examiner's* note** A useful quotation from Aquinas is: 'Now whatever is moved is moved by another … it is therefore impossible that in the same respect and in the same way a thing should be both mover and moved.'

Aquinas' Second Way

21 Why did Aquinas say that nothing could be its own cause?

22 Why can there not, according to Aquinas, be an infinite series of causes?

23 How does Aquinas arrive at the conclusion that God is the first cause?

24 Why is God different from all other beings?

ANSWERS

A1 because this is a logical impossibility, since all things in our world are dependent upon other causes or actions which exist prior to themselves

A2 because this would mean that there was no first cause and so nothing could or would exist; since things *do* exist, there must, of necessity, be a first cause

A3 by means of an inductive leap from the observation that there needs to be a first cause to the claim that only God could fulfil this role

A4 God, unlike other beings, is not caused

***examiner's* note** The argument has popular appeal because it uses evidence which is universally available and which cannot be challenged.

17 ANSWERS

Aquinas' Third Way

Q1 Why did Aquinas believe that it was impossible that all beings should be capable of existing or not existing?

Q2 Which modern scholar said that a necessary being must exist and cannot not exist?

Q3 Identify two scholars who have rejected the concept of necessary existence.

Q4 What quality of God grants him necessary existence?

ANSWERS

A1 if this was the case, then at some point, all beings might cease to exist at once; therefore there must exist a being that is necessary rather than contingent

A2 F. C. Copleston

A3 David Hume and Bertrand Russell

A4 aseity — independence from all other beings

examiner's **note** Aquinas wrote: 'Therefore if everything can not-be then at one time there was nothing in existence … (and) it would have been impossible for anything to have begun to exist and thus even now nothing would be in existence, which is absurd.'

Developing the Cosmological Argument

Q1 Who explained the Cosmological Argument as a 'principle of sufficient reason'?

Q2 What is meant by 'infinite regress'?

Q3 What is the Islamic Kalam Argument?

Q4 Why, according to Leibniz, do items require an explanation for their existence?

ANSWERS

A1 Gottfried Leibniz, in his work *Theodicy*; a sufficient reason is a complete explanation to which nothing further can be added

A2 the notion that one can trace causes back to infinity, without finding, or needing, a beginning or first cause

A3 an argument developed prior to Aquinas, by al-Kindi (c. 870) and al-Ghazali (1058–1111), which states that nothing comes into being without being caused

A4 because we need to establish why there is something rather than nothing; even a book of the principles of geometry needs a complete explanation and cannot be explained simply by a previous book

***examiner's* note** According to Leibniz, the Cosmological Argument depends on establishing that there is a cause for everything which also explains everything.

 **19 ANSWERS**

David Hume's criticisms

Q1 In which book did Hume criticise the Cosmological Argument?

Q2 Why, according to Hume, was Aquinas guilty of an unacceptable leap of logic?

Q3 Why did Hume believe that the notion of a necessary being was an inconsistent one?

Q4 Why did Hume challenge the notion that an explanation for the whole chain had to be found?

ANSWERS

A1 *Dialogues Concerning Natural Religion*

A2 he moved from the need for a first mover to identifying the first mover as God, claiming that only God could fulfil that role

A3 he believed that there was no being the non-existence of which is inconceivable

A4 he argued that to be able to explain the parts should be sufficient; it makes no difference to the nature of things if we can explain only the parts, and not the whole

***examiner's* note** David Hume argued that it was 'a great partiality' to suggest that while everything else needed an explanation, God did not.

Modern criticisms of the Cosmological Argument

Q1 Who argued that it was gratuitous to demand an explanation for the universe?

Q2 What does *reductio ad absurdum* mean? How might it apply to the Cosmological Argument?

Q3 What does it mean for an argument to have perennial value? How might it apply to the Cosmological Argument?

Q4 Who said 'God is simpler than anything we can imagine' and therefore provides the simplest explanation for the universe?

ANSWERS

there is continued debate about whether the argument gives the best explanation for the universe

A1 Bertrand Russell

A2 reduction to an absurdity — a counter-argument which reduces a proposal to absurd conclusions; Russell famously observed that although every person who exists has a mother, it would be absurd to demand a mother for the whole human race

A3 the argument has remained valid throughout the centuries and remains so today; the Cosmological Argument addresses questions of existence which remain perennially valid

A4 Richard Swinburne

***examiner's* note** John Hick maintained that 'the atheistic option that the universe is "just there" is the more economical option'. This follows the principle of Ockham's Razor, i.e. scientific and philosophical theories should be kept as simple as possible.

The Design Argument (1)

21 Why is the Design Argument also called the Teleological Argument?

22 Is the Design Argument *a priori* or *a posteriori*, and why?

23 Who said the argument was 'the most accordant with the common reason of mankind'?

24 What is Aquinas' Fifth Way?

ANSWERS

an argument developed from observation of the nature of beings and items in the universe

A1 teleological comes from *telos*, which means 'end' or 'purpose'; the Design Argument maintains that objects in the universe seem to work towards an end or purpose

A2 *a posteriori* because it is an argument based on empirical evidence

A3 Immanuel Kant

A4 there is beneficial order in the universe and things work to an end or purpose; objects in the universe do not have the intelligence to work towards an end or purpose of their own accord and therefore they are directed by something that does, namely God

***examiner's* note** According to Richard Swinburne: 'So there is our universe. It is characterised by vast, all-persuasive temporal order, the conformity of nature to formula, recorded in the scientific laws formulated by humans.'

The Design Argument (2)

What is meant by the following terms, in relation to the Design Argument:

21 order?

22 benefit?

23 purpose?

24 suitability?

ANSWERS

the argument that the character of the universe suggests it is designed by a supreme intelligence

A1 the universe shows order in the behaviour of objects and laws, e.g. seasonal patterns, sunrise and sunset

A2 the universe provides all that is beneficial and necessary for life; nature provides 14 superfoods, e.g. broccoli, blueberries and wild salmon, which can prevent certain critical illnesses and promote longevity

A3 objects within the universe seem to work towards an end or purpose, e.g. grey whales travel thousands of miles to breed in warmer climates

A4 the order of the universe provides a perfectly suitable environment for human life, e.g. the balance of the atmosphere

***examiner's* note** The heart of the Design Argument is that the delicate balance of the universe is such that the probability of it coming about by chance is far too remote. It has to have had a designer.

(23) ANSWERS

William Paley's analogy

Q1 Outline Paley's analogy.

Q2 Why is the watch an analogy?

Q3 Identify the criticisms of the analogy which Paley anticipates?

Q4 Why does the analogy fail?

ANSWERS

a classic explanation of the Design Argument

A1 if you were walking across a heath and found a watch, you would notice that it has several parts which work together; it appears to have been designed and, if so, there must be a watch-maker

A2 the watch shows evidence of having purpose, design and an end function — just like the universe; the watch is an analogy for the universe

A3 many factors about the watch might count against its design: it may go wrong, or have parts which seem inexplicable

A4 we know that a watch is designed because we have other designed watches to compare with it; however, we do not have another universe, designed or not, to compare with this one

***examiner's* note** Be careful in the exam to avoid re-telling the analogy of the watch in detail. Simply refer to it and concentrate on the issues stemming from it.

(24) **ANSWERS**

Modern Design Arguments

21 What does Swinburne mean by the providential nature of the universe?

22 Why does he consider that this could be proof of the existence of God?

23 What is the Aesthetic Argument?

24 What is the Anthropic Principle?

ANSWERS

many features of the universe appear to demand an explanation, not just its order and structure

A1 the universe contains all that is necessary for human life; natural laws function and help humans to develop

A2 this shows that there is a loving God who cares for his creation

A3 the universe possesses a natural beauty that goes beyond that which is necessary for life; this beauty displays the handicraft of the creator

A4 the reason for the universe is to support human life; evolution and the big bang may be the means that God has employed to create this environment

examiner's note These views can be useful in an exam answer as a contrast to the classical views of Aquinas. Use them particularly in evaluation, but don't get too bogged down in scientific explanations of the world.

Criticisms of the Design Argument

Q1 Why might the Design Argument be criticised for anthropomorphising God?

Q2 What does it mean to say that the universe is religiously ambiguous?

Q3 What reason did John Stuart Mill give for arguing that the creator must be seriously limited in power?

Q4 What did Richard Dawkins mean by saying that natural selection has no purpose in mind?

ANSWERS))

the Design Argument may point to the probability of God, but it is inconclusive as a proof

A1 if we compare God with a human designer, this only emphasises his limitedness and fallibility; it does not support the view of an omnipotent God

A2 that the existence of the universe could be explained in many different ways, not just by reference to God

A3 the existence of evil and suffering

A4 natural selection happens without a predetermined plan and needs no personal direction

***examiner's* note** Dawkins said of natural selection: 'It has no vision, no foresight, no sight at all. If it can be said to play the role of the watchmaker in nature, it is the blind watchmaker.'

(26) ANSWERS

The Ontological Argument

Q1 What type of proof is the Ontological Argument, and why?

Q2 Why is the Ontological Argument a deductive argument?

Q3 In what way does the Ontological Argument use analytic terms?

Q4 What does *de dicto* mean, and how is it relevant to the Ontological Argument?

ANSWERS ❯❯

a classic argument for the existence of God which uses logic and deductive reasoning

A1 it is an *a priori* proof, because it is not based on evidence gathered from empirical observation or experience

A2 because the conclusion is contained within the premises and so it reaches a logically necessary conclusion

A3 the definition of God used in the argument is assumed to be true by definition

A4 'of words' rather than of experience or of the nature of things; the Ontological Argument seeks to establish God's necessary existence *de dicto* — the very word 'God' means that he must and cannot not exist

examiner's **note** Ontological arguments are conceptual in the way that, for example, the propositions constituting the concept of a bachelor imply that every bachelor is male; the propositions constituting the concept of God imply that God exists.

27 **ANSWERS**

Anselm's form of the Ontological Argument (1)

Q1 How did Anselm define God for the purposes of the Ontological Argument?

Q2 Suggest how Anselm's first form of the argument (ch. 2 of *Proslogion*) could be set out in premises and a conclusion.

Q3 Upon what understanding of the nature of God is Anselm's second form of the argument (ch. 3 of *Proslogion*) dependent?

Q4 Explain the concepts of *in re* and *in intellectu* as applied to the Ontological Argument.

ANSWERS

A1 that than which nothing greater can be conceived/thought of

A2 P1: God is the greatest conceivable being; P2: if God exists in the mind alone, a greater being could be imagined to exist both in the mind and in reality; P3: this being would then be greater than God; P4: thus God cannot exist only as an idea in the mind

A3 that God possesses necessary existence since he cannot even be thought of as not existing

A4 *in re* — in reality; *in intellectu* — in the mind/intellect, without real existence; God must exist *in re* and *in intellectu*; God's existence is not imaginary

***examiner's* note** It is a logical contradiction to claim that God does not exist, since any being that has the property of necessary existence could not fail to exist.

Anselm's form of the Ontological Argument (2)

Q1 Who is Anselm's fool?

Q2 How does Anselm use the analogy of a painter?

Q3 How did Anselm understand the notion of existence?

Q4 Why did Gaunilo criticise Anselm's form of the argument?

ANSWERS

A1 the atheist of Psalms 14:1 and 53:1: 'The fool says in his heart, "There is no God." They are corrupt, and their ways are vile.'

A2 a painter imagines what he is going to paint in his mind, but it cannot be said to truly exist until he has painted it; in the same way, God cannot exist in the mind only

A3 as a perfection necessary to be that than which nothing greater can be conceived

A4 because it effectively defined God into existence by claiming that that which is perfect must exist; if this argument were applied to things in the world, it would lead to an absurd conclusion

***examiner's* note** Remember that Gaunilo was not an atheist. He believed in God but objected to the form of Anselm's reasoning.

Responding to Gaunilo's criticisms

Q1 How did Anselm respond to Gaunilo's criticism?

Q2 Outline Alvin Plantinga's response to Gaunilo's criticism.

Q3 Suggest another criticism of Anselm's reasoning concerning existence *in re* and *in intellectu*.

Q4 Suggest another criticism of Gaunilo's response.

ANSWERS

Gaunilo's response was outlined in his work *On Behalf of the Fool*

A1 Gaunilo had tried to apply his reasoning to a contingent thing, when it was intended only to apply to the necessary being of God

A2 the most perfect island is an incoherent example, since it has no intrinsic maximum, while God can be no more perfect

A3 Anselm assumes that existence *in re* is intrinsically better than existence *in intellectu*; conceivably some things would be better to exist *in intellectu* only, e.g. murderers

A4 contingent things are subjectively perfect; one person's idea of a perfect island is not necessarily the same as another's

***examiner's* note** Gaunilo attempted to use a *reductio ad absurdum* to undermine Anselm's reasoning, but his own argument can be reduced to an absurdity itself.

(30) ANSWERS

Descartes' form of the argument

Q1 What form of the argument does Descartes support?

Q2 Why did Descartes favour the Ontological Argument over other arguments for the existence of God?

Q3 How did Descartes illustrate his form of the argument?

Q4 Why did Descartes believe that the idea of a perfect being proved the existence of a perfect being?

ANSWERS

Descartes revived the argument which had been devastatingly criticised by Aquinas 400 years earlier

A1 the necessary existence of God; existence is part of the definition of God and cannot be separated from his nature

A2 as a rationalist philosopher, Descartes rejected the empirical arguments as unreliable

A3 the existence of God belongs analytically to him in the same way as three angles belong to a triangle

A4 if, as an imperfect being, he could conceive of a perfect being, the perfect being must exist to put that idea in the mind of the imperfect being

***examiner's* note** Descartes does not rely on a definition of God but on the notion that God's existence is inferred directly from the fact that necessary existence is contained in the idea of a supremely perfect being.

(31) **ANSWERS**

Existence as a predicate

Q1 Why did Kant object to the reasoning of the Ontological Argument?

Q2 Outline Kant's critique of the argument.

Q3 How did Bertrand Russell criticise the argument?

Q4 Suggest a counter-argument to Kant's and Russell's objections.

ANSWERS

a predicate is a defining characteristic of a thing or being, which can be possessed or lacked

A1 because it assumed that existence is predicated of a thing

A2 the existence of a thing must be established before we can say anything about its characteristics; if God exists, he is supremely perfect, but it is illogical to say that God is supremely perfect and therefore must exist

A3 existence is used to indicate that a thing occupies time and space, e.g. the statement 'cows are brown' tells us something about cows; that cows are brown and exist adds nothing to our understanding of them

A4 'exists' is the only predicate of a thing which rules out the possession of other properties; that is, God cannot be supremely perfect if he does not possess the property of existence

***examiner's* note** Kant illustrated his argument by observing that 100 thalers (a unit of currency) which existed in the mind was no different from 100 thalers in reality.

(32) ANSWERS

Modern applications of the argument

21 Outline Plantinga's notion of possible worlds.

22 What, for Plantinga, are the implications of God having necessary existence?

23 How does Norman Malcolm apply necessary existence to the argument?

24 Suggest why the argument might be considered to support an anti-realist understanding of the existence of God.

ANSWERS

these applications focus on the logical structure of the Ontological Argument

A1 since we can conceive of any number of alternative worlds in which things may be different, there must be any number of possible worlds

A2 if God has necessary existence and is maximally excellent in one world, then he must exist and possess these characteristics in all worlds

A3 since God cannot contingently exist, his existence is either necessary or impossible; God's existence is therefore necessary, since it would be contradictory to say that a perfect being did not exist

A4 the claims in the argument are already held to be true by believers, and may be considered subjectively, not objectively, true

examiner's **note** The notion of the argument as an anti-realist one can be related to language game theory, a non-cognitive way of understanding how the language of a particular discipline, belief system or world view can survive charges of meaninglessness.

(33) ANSWERS

The argument from religious experience (1)

21 What is meant by a religious experience?

22 What is a private religious experience?

23 What is a public religious experience?

24 On what empirical principle is the argument for religious experience based?

ANSWERS

an attempt to prove the existence of God from direct experience of him

A1 an experience that is best explained as a direct encounter with God

A2 an experience that is unique to the individual who has it, such as a dream, and to which they give religious significance

A3 an experience that is available to many people — such as a beautiful sunset — to which some people may ascribe religious significance

A4 the principle that experience is reliable and can be used as the basis for drawing conclusions about the world

examiner's note Richard Swinburne argues that an omnipotent and perfectly good creator would choose to interact with human beings, and that religious experience therefore tips the balance in favour of God's existence.

The argument from religious experience (2)

Q1 What is the principle of testimony?

Q2 What is the principle of credulity?

Q3 Why is the character of the experient said to be important when evaluating the argument?

Q4 Why might this not be as significant as some would claim?

ANSWERS

A1 'in the absence of special considerations the experiences of others are (probably) as they report them' (Swinburne)

A2 'If it seems to a subject that X is present, then probably X is present' (Swinburne)

A3 if the experient is known to suffer from delusions, addictions, psychological illnesses or has a reputation for untruthfulness, the reliability of the accounts may be questioned

A4 according to Brian Davies, 'the truth of a belief is not affected by the factors that bring the belief about', i.e. even if the circumstances are questionable, the experience itself is not necessarily invalid

***examiner's* note** Essays on religious experience as an argument for the existence of God should consist of more than just descriptions of types of experiences.

35 **ANSWERS**

The argument from religious experience (3)

Q1 How is the term 'blik' relevant to the argument from religious experience?

Q2 Explain Wittgenstein's principle of 'seeing-as'.

Q3 Outline two arguments in support of religious experience as proof for the existence of God.

Q4 Outline two weaknesses of the argument.

ANSWERS ❯❯

'levitations, ecstasies, trances and the like... prove nothing' (Clifton Wolters)

A1 a blik is an unfalsifiable way of looking at the world; all interpretations of religious experience could be thought to be bliks — they can never therefore be disproved as evidence for the existence of God

A2 each person perceives an experience differently; what one might interpret as a religious experience, others might interpret as non-religious

A3 it is reasonable to assume that if God exists he would want to make himself known to his people; God may be the simplest explanation

A4 there are no tests to verify the experience; the testimony of religious believers may be biased; if there is a God, why doesn't everyone experience him?

***examiner's* note** In examination answers use philosophical grounds to support the argument from religious experience.

The nature of religious experience (1)

Q1 What is meant by 'numinous'?

Q2 What is a conversion experience?

Q3 What is a corporate experience?

Q4 What is a charismatic experience?

ANSWERS

an experience in which the experient believes he or she has had a direct encounter with the divine

A1 coined by Rudolph Otto from the Latin *numen*, it describes the feeling of being in the presence of something wholly other and beyond regular human experience

A2 an experience in which the experient's life is changed by an encounter with the divine, leading him or her to change religious beliefs or to adopt them for the first time

A3 an experience of the divine which takes place when a large group are gathered together for the purpose of worship or in expectation of a divine revelation or encounter

A4 an experience of the Holy Spirit such as speaking in tongues, prophecy, words of knowledge and interpretation of tongues

examiner's **note** Use these key terms in context to gain credit.

The nature of religious experience (2)

21 Outline the key ideas associated with William James.

22 What is the Alastair Hardy Research Unit?

23 Identify two biblical religious experiences.

24 What kind of proof is an argument for the existence of God based on religious experience?

ANSWERS

interest in religious experience was revived in the latter half of the twentieth century

A1 he observed that religious experiences draw on a range of emotions, such as happiness, fear and wonder, but are directed at the divine, leading to feelings of reverence, joy and a desire to belong to God

A2 the religious experience research unit in Oxford; studies here conclude that a majority of the population have had a spiritual experience

A3 conversion: Saul/Paul (Acts 9); Pentecost and speaking in tongues (Acts 2); Moses and the burning bush (Exodus 3); the Transfiguration (Mark 9)

A4 an *a posteriori* proof, based on the most direct kind of experience

***examiner's* note** Schliermacher defined a religious experience as one that offered a sense of the ultimate, an awareness of wholeness, a consciousness of infiniteness and finiteness, and a feeling of absolute dependence.

(**38**) **ANSWERS**

William James: four characteristics of religious experience

21 What is meant by 'ineffability'?

22 What is meant by 'noetic'?

23 What is meant by 'transiency'?

24 What is meant by 'passivity'?

ANSWERS

the relationship between God and the experient is a key element of religious experience

A1 the experience cannot be described in words, but can only be felt by the person who experiences it

A2 the experience communicates truths which cannot be communicated through the regular channels; it unveils or reveals some new insight

A3 the experience lasts for a short time only

A4 experients often feel as if they are being controlled by a higher being or power, and the direction of the experience is completely out of their hands

***examiner's* note** Richard Swinburne identified three types of private religious experience —— those that can be described using normal language, those that cannot, and those in which the individual is directly aware of God —— and two types of public experience —— those in which God is identified in a public way and those that occur as a result of extraordinary public events.

Mysticism

21 Identify the common features of a mystical experience.

22 Name two famous mystics.

23 Distinguish between introvertive and objective mystical experiences.

24 Why are accounts of mystical experiences open to criticism?

ANSWERS

an experience in which the ultimate reality is vividly encountered

A1 a sense of union with the divine; a sense of separateness from God; time is transcended; something is revealed to the experient; a sense of well-being

A2 Mother Julian of Norwich; St Teresa of Avila

A3 introvertive: mystics look inwards on their experience and understand their oneness with the divine; objective: the experience of the mystic is like that of the poet, contemplating outward circumstances

A4 because they can be faked; they can generate a sense of spiritual superiority; they are open to alternative interpretations

examiner's **note** Clifton Wolters writes: 'The Christian mystic is regarded as one who has been raised to a high degree of contemplative prayer.'

Miracles

Q1 Who defined a miracle as 'a transgression of a law of nature by a particular volition of the deity'?

Q2 What are the three main characteristics of a miracle?

Q3 What is 'natural law'?

Q4 Distinguish between a strong and weak miracle.

ANSWERS ❯❯

A1 David Hume in *An Enquiry Concerning Human Understanding*

A2 it is a violation of a law of nature; it has a purpose or justification; it is open to the possibility of a religious interpretation

A3 that which happens regularly within nature; the view that everything works to a particular design and for a particular purpose, and does not act irregularly or unpredictably

A4 a strong miracle involves a violation of a natural law; a weak miracle could be an event which is given religious significance

***examiner's* note** Always begin an examination answer on miracles by defining your terms. Remember that the word 'miracle' refers to an action by God. If there is no God, there can be no miracles.

Miracles: Thomas Aquinas

Q1 What, according to Aquinas, are the three main kinds of miracle?

Q2 What did Aquinas mean by an interventionist God?

Q3 Why have some scholars suggested that Aquinas' views contradict biblical teaching?

Q4 What unfounded assumption did Aquinas make about human understanding of natural laws?

ANSWERS))

Aquinas took the traditional biblical view and suggested miracles occur when God breaks natural laws

A1 actions done by God (a) which nature could never do; (b) which nature could do, but not in that order; (c) which nature could do, but which God does without reference to nature

A2 God intervenes in a random fashion, performing miracles unexpectedly and inconsistently

A3 since the scriptures depict God as a loving father, he should act fairly and not just perform miracles for the lucky few

A4 Aquinas argued that God breaks natural laws to perform miracles; his wrongful assumption is that humans know every natural law, and therefore know when God is breaking such a law

***examiner's* note** Aquinas' views are very useful in the examination, particularly in contrast with David Hume's.

 **ANSWERS**

Miracles: philosophical issues

Q1 Who said that 'a coincidence can be taken religiously as a sign and called a miracle'?

Q2 Why is subjectivity a problem when talking about miracles?

Q3 How would a realist view miracles?

Q4 How would an anti-realist view miracles?

ANSWERS »

A1 R. F. Holland in *Religion and Understanding*

A2 whether or not an action is regarded as a miracle will depend on the individual (subjective) view of the person experiencing it — a religious believer may see the event as a miracle, while an atheist may see it as a coincidence

A3 a realist is concerned with objective truth and would argue that miracles do not happen since the only evidence for them is subjective

A4 an anti-realist looks at subjective truth and would argue that miracles are true for those who believe them to be so, but that does not make them true for everyone

examiner's note Avoid the temptation in the examination to retell Holland's story of the boy and the express train; examiners have all read it hundreds of times before.

43 ANSWERS

Miracles: David Hume

21 In which book did Hume outline his criticisms of miracles?

22 What is meant by the term 'testimony'?

23 In what ways did Hume criticise the reliability of the testimonies of witnesses to miracles?

24 What did Hume mean by his reference to 'ignorant and barbarous nations'?

ANSWERS

Hume's views are rooted in his atheism and belief that accounts of miracles can never be reliable

A1 in *An Enquiry Concerning Human Understanding*

A2 a testimony is a claim which a person makes, believing it to be true

A3 Hume questioned whether there had ever been a sufficient number of intelligent and reliable witnesses to a miracle, and suggested that those who claimed to have seen miracles were those people who were prone to look for them

A4 Hume believed that reports of miracles came from nations where the people were less well educated than in what was then the developed world

***examiner's* note** You will almost certainly have to include the views of Hume in an exam answer on miracles. However, don't let his views dominate the entire essay — his opinion is just one of several important ones you need to be familiar with.

Miracles: testimony

21 Why did Hume question the reliability of testimony concerning miracles from different religious traditions?

22 What is the principle of Ockham's Razor?

23 What is Swinburne's 'principle of testimony'?

24 Explain Swinburne's 'principle of credulity'.

ANSWERS

A1 Hume believed that testimonies of miracles from different religious traditions cancel each other out, since they could not all be right; therefore, all testimony is unreliable

A2 the principle that the simpler the explanation, the better it is

A3 the principle that people, generally, tell the truth

A4 we should be willing to accept the truth of what people say, unless we have really compelling reasons to doubt them

***examiner's* note** The principles of testimony and credulity can also be applied to accounts of religious experience.

Miracles in the Bible

21 Why, according to the Gospels, did Jesus Christ perform miracles?

22 Which modern scholar argued that there must always be a reason for God's miraculous intervention?

23 Which scholar advocated 'demythologising' the Bible?

24 What did he mean by this?

ANSWERS

the Bible is the prime source for accounts of miracles and an interpretation of them

A1 Jesus performed miracles to encourage and strengthen the faith of believers and to show the love and power of God

A2 Richard Swinburne wrote: 'If a god intervened in the natural order to make a feather land here rather than there, for no deep, ultimate purpose…these events would not naturally be described as miracles'

A3 Rudolph Bultmann

A4 Bultmann claimed that the modern mind could not understand biblical myths and advocated that they should be removed (demythologised) so that a clearer picture of the biblical message would be available for the modern age

examiner's **note** It is useful to refer to biblical miracles, but don't just tell the story.

The nature of evil

Q1 What is natural evil?

Q2 What is moral evil?

Q3 Give one example of natural evil and one example of moral evil.

Q4 What is a theodicy?

ANSWERS

evil is the apparent going wrong of something which is inherently good

A1 the apparent going wrong of the natural world, or conditions within it, which gives rise to human or animal suffering

A2 morally wrongful human actions, either by commission or omission

A3 natural evil: earthquakes, volcanoes, floods, droughts; moral evil: murder, wars, rape, damaging actions against the environment or humanity

A4 an attempt to justify the existence of a loving God in the face of evil

examiner's **note** These terms form the basis of discussion concerning this topic. You must know and understand the difference between natural and moral evil because they raise different problems. The first is, in many ways, outside human control; the second is well within human control.

(47) **ANSWERS**

The problem of evil

Q1 Who said 'Either God cannot prevent evil, or He will not'?

Q2 What is meant by omnipotent, omniscient, and omnibenevolent?

Q3 Why is the existence of evil a problem for religious believers?

Q4 Who put forward the idea of the inconsistent triad in his book *Evil and Omnipotence,* and what is it?

ANSWERS

the problem of evil challenges the notion of an all-powerful God

A1 Augustine

A2 all-powerful, all-knowing, and perfectly good, or all-loving

A3 for many religious believers, God is all-knowing, all-powerful and all-loving and, as such, should be able to prevent evil and suffering; however, since evil and suffering exist, does God exist, and if he does, does he possess the characteristics attributed to him by classical theism?

A4 J. L. Mackie; a group of three contradictory claims — God's omnipotence, God's omnibenevolence and the existence of evil

examiner's **note** The essence of the problem of evil is not that God does evil but that he cannot or will not prevent it; this calls into question the nature of belief in such a God.

The Augustinian theodicy (1)

Q1 On which book of the Old Testament did Augustine base much of his theodicy?

Q2 Augustine described God's initial creation as good. What does 'good' mean in this context?

Q3 How did Augustine describe evil?

Q4 According to Augustine, how did evil enter the world?

ANSWERS

a soul-deciding solution to the problem of evil, offered by Augustine (354 CE–430 CE)

A1 Genesis, chapters 1–3

A2 free from defect, or perfect

A3 as the privation, or lack, of good

A4 it entered when beings of free will (angels and humans) chose to reject God and settle for lesser good; when humans rejected God, they rejected his perfection, therefore the perfection of the created world has been flawed; moral evil came about when humanity received the knowledge of good and evil, and chose to reject God's goodness — as a result, all humans are now tainted with sin

examiner's **note** Augustine based his theodicy firmly in the creation story in Genesis chapters 1–3. You must familiarise yourself with this narrative in order to appreciate the theodicy fully.

49 **ANSWERS**

The Augustinian theodicy (2)

21 According to this view, why does God not intervene to prevent suffering?

22 Why did Augustine think God punishes sinful humans?

23 What hope did he think humans have?

24 In what sense might it be said that suffering is essential for human survival?

ANSWERS

for Augustine a good God must, of necessity, also be a just God

A1 Augustine saw suffering as a punishment and consequence of sin

A2 God is just and must, therefore, ensure that justice is done; sin is wrongfulness which must be punished

A3 although humans deserve the ultimate punishment of hell, God offers forgiveness and salvation through belief in Jesus Christ; all who believe in him will be saved

A4 without some suffering, humanity and the universe would be static

***examiner's* note** You need to understand the importance of the death and resurrection of Jesus Christ to Augustine's theodicy. The New Testament teaches that those who believe in Jesus will be saved, since his death is seen as the punishment for their sins (see, for example, John 3:16). For this reason, the theodicy may be considered unacceptable to non-Christians.

The Irenaean theodicy

21 According to this theodicy, why did God make humans and the world imperfectly?

22 How did Irenaeus think that humans are supposed to develop perfectly?

23 Why did he think that God gave humans free will?

24 Which modern scholars have developed the Irenaean theodicy?

ANSWERS

a soul-making solution, earlier than that of Augustine, and less dependent on biblical traditions

A1 in order that humans could grow and develop into perfection over time, in part due to their experience of pain and suffering

A2 humans will develop through cooperation with the will and guidance of God in order to close the distance of knowledge between them

A3 free will enables humans to choose between good and evil and to make choices which influence creation and other human beings; they do not have to follow God if they do not want to

A4 John Hick and Richard Swinburne

examiner's **note** Many students make the mistake of thinking that Irenaeus and Augustine lived at the same time. Irenaeus died 150 years before Augustine was born.

 **51** ANSWERS

Problems with the Irenaean theodicy

21 The Irenaean theodicy may suggest that everyone goes to heaven. Why is that a problem?

22 What is wrong with the justification that suffering enables humans to develop?

23 Who said, of a child dying of cancer: 'If God is this kind of agent, he cannot justify his actions'?

24 What is the problem of the severity of human suffering?

ANSWERS

the theodicy allows for evolution and development but has difficulties over fairness and justice

A1 if everyone goes to heaven, then this is neither fair nor just; there would be no point in leading a good life

A2 not all suffering produces good consequences — much suffering produces only misery

A3 D. Z. Phillips in *The Concept of Prayer*

A4 much human suffering seems too great compared to the good, if any, that comes from it

***examiner's* note** In the examination, remember that these criticisms are powerful, but they do not disprove the Irenaean theodicy. The theodicy represents a way of looking at the world and human experience but is effectively a means of interpreting the universe in a way which is compatible with belief in God.

Evil, God and humanity

Q1 What does the term 'epistemic distance' mean?

Q2 Why is epistemic distance important?

Q3 What is the counterfactual hypothesis?

Q4 Why is counterfactual hypothesis an unsatisfactory notion?

ANSWERS

A1 the distance God keeps from humans in order not to overwhelm them; it is a distance of knowledge

A2 it enables humans to choose freely, without being influenced too much by God

A3 the notion that God should intervene to make everything right by removing evil or the consequences of it

A4 it is unsatisfactory because if God made everything right, humans would not be able to develop freely; it is logically impossible that he should make free beings who can only choose the good

examiner's **note** A good examination answer will address the reasons why God cannot act freely — the notion of epistemic distance and the counterfactual hypothesis highlight the difficulties an all-loving and powerful God might face.

Process theology

Q1 Name two scholars associated with the development of process theodicy.

Q2 How does process theodicy regard the creation of the universe?

Q3 According to this theodicy, what is God's place in the universe and what is his relationship with humanity?

Q4 What does the expression 'God is the fellow sufferer who understands' mean?

ANSWERS

a modern solution that redefines the traditional concept of God's omnipotence

A1 A. N. Whitehead and David Griffin

A2 the universe is an uncreated, developing process; God started off the evolutionary process which led to the development of humanity

A3 God is part of the universe and is bound by natural laws; he is not omnipotent, but attempts to persuade the universe towards the good — humans are free to accept or reject God

A4 when evil occurs, God suffers, as humans do, because he is part of the same universe; he cannot change natural laws, but must take some responsibility for starting the process

***examiner's* note** To understand this theodicy, you need to put aside any religious ideas you have about God and approach it in a fresh light. God does not dwell aloof from the universe, but is part of it and subject to the processes of it.

Evil and human freedom

Q1 What is meant by the expression 'the world is a logically necessary environment for the exercise of human choices'?

Q2 Why is free will so necessary?

Q3 Why would a loving God allow humanity the freedom to choose?

Q4 Who said of God: 'The less he allows men to bring about large-scale horrors, the less freedom and responsibility he gives them'?

ANSWERS

a key idea which underlies all theodicies, that human beings are free to make moral choices

A1 the world provides freedom in the form of choices that produce both good and bad results

A2 above and beyond the ability to make moral choices, free will is necessary so as to enable humans to choose to accept or reject God

A3 God wants humans to choose to love him; he does not want to force them to do so, since such love would not be genuine

A4 Richard Swinburne in *The Existence of God* (1979)

examiner's **note** This is a powerful argument and has some basis in the scriptures and in non-Christian traditions. God does not force himself upon anyone, but waits patiently for them to choose him.

The Bible and creation

21 What is a fundamentalist interpretation of the creation of the world?

22 What is a liberal interpretation of the creation of the world?

23 What is a traditional or conservative interpretation of the creation of the world?

24 Why may there be conflicts between religious believers who hold these different positions?

ANSWERS

these two interpretations of the nature of the universe are often thought to conflict

A1   the belief that all claims made in scripture are literally true

A2   the belief that scriptures are not literally true, but contain religious truth, conveyed through symbol, myth or other literary devices

A3   the belief that there is spiritual truth in scripture, but parts of it need to be reinterpreted in the light of new discoveries, e.g. scientific, historical or archaeological information

A4   fundamentalists may claim that suggesting that any part of scripture is not literally true undermines the truthfulness of the whole divine revelation; liberal or conservative believers may suggest that it is naïve to deny verifiable information revealed by scholarship

***examiner's* note** You need to know key terminology for this topic. It is not enough just to learn a basic narrative version of the Genesis accounts of creation.

Religious interpretations of the origin of the world (1)

21 Who was James Ussher and what did he propose?

22 What view of creation does the following claim support: 'The universe was formed at God's command, so that what is seen was not made out of what was visible' (Hebrews 11:3)?

23 What is the status of human beings in a typical religious interpretation of the world?

24 Why is the anthropic principle useful for a religious interpretation of the world?

ANSWERS

a religious interpretation traditionally sees creation as the act of an interventionist God

A1 he became Bishop of Armagh in 1625 and, working with the Old Testament genealogies, reached the conclusion that creation took place in 4004 BCE

A2 creation ex *nihilo*; God's word alone had creative power to bring something out of nothing

A3 they are the climax and goal of creation, in the image of God, and they are to have dominion over the rest of creation

A4 it asserts that the carefully balanced order of the world can be best explained by complementary, not conflicting, scientific and religious interpretations

***examiner's* note** Although there is some overlap with the Design Argument here, take care not to turn an answer on religion and science into a Design Argument essay.

57 ANSWERS

Religious interpretations of the origin of the world (2)

21 What is meant by 'evolutionary creationism'?

22 What is meant by 'evolutionary mysticism'?

23 What is meant by 'age-day flat creationism'?

24 What is meant by 'young-earth creationism'?

ANSWERS ▶▶

A1 that God created the universe through the process of evolution

A2 that there is some mystic meaning behind the evolutionary process

A3 that creation occurred through divine intervention in separate acts of God over a long period of time

A4 that creation occurred through divine intervention over a period of 144 hours, 6,000–8,000 years ago

***examiner's* note** Using these terms will lift your answer to a more scholarly level. They will help to show that you understand that not all religious interpretations are the same.

(58) ANSWERS

Scientific interpretations of the origin of the world

21 Outline what is meant by the 'big bang'.

22 Outline what is meant by 'evolution'.

23 What did the Belgian priest Georges Lemaître and the astronomer Edwin Hubble propose?

24 Why are scientific interpretations of the world thought to be in conflict with religious interpretations?

ANSWERS

such explanations are thought to be complete without referring to divine activity or agency

A1 between 10 and 20 billion years ago, a cosmic explosion hurled matter into space and laid the foundations of the universe

A2 all living beings are descended from common ancestors and have evolved in response to natural competition for survival

A3 in 1927, Georges Lemaître proposed that the universe began with the explosion of a primeval atom; in 1929, Edwin Hubble found that distant galaxies travel away from us at speeds proportional to their distance

A4 they do not include the possibility of the universe having intrinsic meaning; humans have no significance outside their evolutionary development; there is no moral imperative on humans to recognise a personal creator

***examiner's* note** Student summaries of the big bang are frequently weak. Make sure you learn a full and accurate version.

(59) ANSWERS

The origin of the world: key ideas

Q1 Which ideas are associated with Richard Dawkins?

Q2 Which ideas are associated with Teilhard de Chardin?

Q3 What is the second law of thermodynamics?

Q4 Why is the probability of a non-directed creation often said to be too low?

ANSWERS ▶▶

key ideas from both perspectives are vital to create a balanced argument

A1 any designer/creator must be 'a blind watchmaker'; religious interpretations are based on myths; religious ideas are intellectually degrading

A2 he aimed most significantly to unify Christian theology with theories of evolution; he saw humanity as heading for an Omega point, which would lead to a new state of unity based intrinsically upon the spirit of the earth

A3 the universe began in a highly ordered, energy-packed state, but over time has become disordered and its energy has dissipated

A4 because the conditions necessary for life on earth are so precise that it is utterly improbable that they have come about by chance

***examiner's* note** It has been said that the likelihood of life beginning by chance is about as great as a hurricane blowing through a scrapyard and assembling a Boeing 747.

Atheism

Q1 Distinguish between strong and weak atheism.

Q2 What is meant by agnosticism?

Q3 Suggest three reasons why someone may be an atheist.

Q4 Why may atheism be claimed to be philosophically more reliable than theism?

ANSWERS

the belief that there is no God

A1 weak atheism is essentially scepticism, possibly in response to the problem of evil, or the unreliability of evidence supporting belief in God; strong atheism is the explicitly held belief that God does not exist

A2 the view that it is not possible to be certain of the existence or non-existence of God

A3 bereavement or other personal suffering; rejection of the mythological concepts associated with belief in God; a belief that science holds the answers to all questions of existence and meaning

A4 on the basis that the claims made by theism cannot be supported by verifiable empirical evidence

***examiner's* note** An agnostic could be open to the possibility of knowledge leading to belief, without being able to say what it would take to make that move.

 **ANSWERS**

Critiques of religion

21 Identify the key features of a critique of religion.

22 What is a functionalist critique of religion?

23 What is a projectionist critique of religion?

24 Why is a critique of religion not necessarily an atheistic argument for the non-existence of God?

ANSWERS

critical analyses of religious belief and practice

A1 the characteristics of religious belief and practice are explained by reference to non-theistic features of human experience

A2 a functionalist critique identifies the function religion serves within society or in the life of the individual

A3 a projectionist critique identifies the way in which religion serves as a projection of human emotional and psychological needs

A4 the existence of God and the practice of religion can be mutually exclusive; it is not unreasonable to suggest that religion is a man-made system, and that God transcends all religious practices and institutions

***examiner's* note** Students often confuse definitions of atheism and critiques of religious belief. Although critiques are invariably offered by atheistic thinkers, they are not interchangeable.

Sociological critiques

21 Outline Durkheim's theory of religion.

22 Identify one strength and one weakness of the theory.

23 Why did Karl Marx argue that 'the first requisite for the happiness of the people is the abolition of religion'?

24 Suggest a counter-argument to Marx's critique of religion.

ANSWERS

functionalist theories of religion that identify the function religion serves within society

A1 religion functions in society to unite and preserve the community: Durkheim likened a religious community worshipping God to a primitive clan which worships a totem that symbolises the unity of the clan

A2 strength: religious believers would accept that corporate elements of religion are important; weakness: religious believers have often rejected society or worked actively to change it

A3 Marx believed that religion prevented people from rebelling against oppression; it left them alienated and helpless

A4 Marx assumed that religion was a stagnating influence, whereas it can be used to bring about change and release the oppressed

***examiner's* note** Marx is also well known for describing religion as 'the opiate of the people'.

Psychological critiques

21 Why did Freud call religion 'a universal neurosis'?

22 How did Freud explain the origins of religious belief?

23 How did Jung's ideas about religion differ from those of Freud?

24 Why might a psychological critique of religion be convincing?

ANSWERS

psychological critiques of religion are most commonly associated with Freud and Jung

A1 because it was an illusion which bound believers into obsessional ways of thinking and acting

A2 as lying in the primitive horde; the father is overthrown, but the subsequent guilt of the sons leads them to elevate his memory and to worship him

A3 Jung also held that religion is an experience of the collective unconscious but, unlike Freud, believed that religion is necessary for personal growth

A4 because many religious believers may acknowledge that religious belief is something upon which they are knowingly dependent

***examiner's* note** You may find it useful to extract some information on these theories from an A-level Psychology textbook.

Dawkins and anti-theism

Q1 What is anti-theism?

Q2 Why does Dawkins suggest that a religious upbringing leads to child abuse?

Q3 What is the title of Dawkins' book in which he outlines his anti-theistic position?

Q4 What is a meme?

ANSWERS

A1   the position adopted, usually by strong atheists, that belief in God leads to dangerous outcomes and intellectually undermining claims about the world

A2   because the parents' beliefs are ascribed to the child, who is in no position to choose for him- or herself

A3   *The God Delusion* (2006)

A4   a meme (term coined by Dawkins) is analogous to a gene, determining our intellectual characteristics, as a gene determines physical ones

***examiner's* note**   Richard Dawkins held the Charles Simonyi Chair in the Public Understanding of Science at Oxford University between 1995 and 2008. His work came to prominence with the publication of *The Selfish Gene* in 1976.

(65) ANSWERS

Moral critiques

Q1 Why might religion be thought to be opposed to morality?

Q2 Why might religious morality be thought to undermine human freedom?

Q3 How might the story of Abraham and Isaac (Genesis 22) be used to support this view?

Q4 How might the parable of the Good Samaritan (Luke 10) support this view?

ANSWERS

a critique of religion based on the claim that religion undermines moral behaviour or makes unreasonable moral demands

A1 because religious believers are committed to obedience to moral commands that may be opposed to a common understanding of what is good

A2 because humans are not free to make their own moral choices if they believe that God requires them to act in a particular way

A3 to explain the story as a test of Abraham's faith is not acceptable to many thinkers

A4 those who did not help the injured man were religious officials

***examiner's* note** A moral critique of religion also serves as a critique of the link between religion and morality, which may be applicable to your study of Ethics.

Other challenges to theism

Q1 What is meant by 'saving theism by adding hypotheses'?

Q2 How does J. Wisdom's parable of the gardener support atheism?

Q3 Explain Richard Dawkins' statement: 'I am against religion because it teaches us to be satisfied with not understanding the world.'

Q4 Explain Ludwig Feuerbach's claim: 'Whenever morality is based on theology…the most immoral…things can be justified.'

ANSWERS ▶▶

many influential philosophers have given atheistic interpretations of the world and human experience

A1 making theism increasingly complex in order to defend its central tenets, e.g. belief in God extends to beliefs in miracles, the afterlife, angels etc.

A2 by observing that theists do not recognise overwhelming challenges to their faith, but qualify their beliefs until what is left is meaningless

A3 Dawkins believes that a theistic explanation of the world stops people from exploring the world and finding out more about it

A4 a characteristic critique of religion based on the dangers of divine command teaching; if religious believers think that God has commanded something, however atrocious, they are compelled to perform that action

***examiner's* note** Another useful quotation comes from the writer Karen Armstrong: 'Religion is not a nice thing. It is potentially a very dangerous thing because it involves a heady complex of emotions, desires, yearnings and fears.'

 **67** **ANSWERS**

Life after death

21 What reason might a Christian have for believing in life after death?

22 Why might non-Christians still hope for an afterlife?

23 What evidence may be offered for an afterlife?

24 What essential problems underlie belief in an afterlife?

ANSWERS

A1 the New Testament promises eternal life to all who accept Jesus

A2 if they are of another faith, they may still believe that God will guarantee them an afterlife; someone with no religious faith may still believe that personal identity does not depend on the physical body

A3 remembered lives, paranormal experiences, a sense of the presence of those who have died still with their loved ones

A4 lack of evidence and the impossibility of verification

examiner's **note** Richard Dawkins argues: 'We should seek immortality in reproduction, but if you contribute to the world's culture…it may live on intact, long after your genes have dissolved in the common pool.' .

The immortality of the soul (1)

21 What, according to Plato, was the aim of the soul?

22 Explain Kant's claim: 'The *summum bonum* is only possible on the presupposition of the immortality of the soul.'

23 What did Aquinas believe that the soul did for the physical body?

24 What did Aquinas mean by the Beatific Vision?

ANSWERS

A1 to break free of the physical world and return to the intelligible realm where it was pre-existent

A2 to achieve the highest good — virtue crowned with happiness — it is necessary that God ensures that the soul survives the death of the body in order to justify morality

A3 the soul animates the body — it gives it life

A4 the highest joy and the unchanging, unending vision of God; eternal life for believers

***examiner's* note** Aquinas was not, strictly speaking, a dualist. He believed that for the soul to have a personal identity, to be an individual, it needed unity with a physical body.

The immortality of the soul (2)

21 What is substance dualism?

22 Outline Descartes' argument for the dualistic nature of human beings.

23 What is property dualism?

24 Suggest one argument in favour of dualism and one against it.

ANSWERS

theories of the soul are also linked to the important relationship between mind and body

A1 the belief that there are two kinds of substance, the body and mind; mind is simple and indivisible, and body composite and divisible

A2 Descartes observed that while he could doubt material existence, he could not doubt that he had a mind; hence, the physical and non-physical are distinct substances with distinct properties

A3 the belief that mental and physical properties are distinct and cannot be reduced to each other

A4 in favour: we identify and describe people by non-physical and physical characteristics; against: the existence of a meaningful non-physical aspect of the personality is untestable and hence unverifiable

examiner's note You do not need to cite dates for philosophers, but make sure that you have an awareness of their chronology.

The resurrection of the body

Q1 What is the difference between resurrection and resuscitation?

Q2 In what ways was Jesus Christ like and different from a human after the Resurrection?

Q3 Identify the philosophical principles which may underlie resurrection.

Q4 How did Paul describe the resurrection event in 1 Corinthians 15?

ANSWERS

a biblical view, based on the Resurrection of Jesus Christ

A1 resurrection is the re-creation by God of the human individual after death; resuscitation is reviving a person, e.g. after a heart attack

A2 Jesus had a physical body which could be seen and touched, but could appear and disappear at will (Luke 24)

A3 monism — that body and soul are a single entity; behaviourism/materialism — the belief that we can only speak meaningfully about what is physical and observable

A4 'For the trumpet will sound, and the dead will be raised imperishable and we shall be changed' (1 Corinthians 15:52)

***examiner's* note** Those who support the resurrection of the body largely do so on the basis that it is meaningless to speak of body and soul as separate entities, as this is not consistent with our experience.

71 ANSWERS

The replica theory

Q1 Which scholar proposed the replica theory? Briefly explain the theory.

Q2 Why is age and appearance a problem for resurrection?

Q3 In what sense could a replica be the same person?

Q4 Identify two problems with this theory.

ANSWERS

A1 John Hick; if someone dies and then appears in a new place, it is meaningful to call this replica the same person

A2 it raises a problem concerning the state of the body at resurrection — how old will it be, will it look the same, will physical defects still exist?

A3 Hick said that God is all-powerful and could create a replica body complete with individual memories and characteristics

A4 if God can make one replica, he can make multiple replicas; which, then, is the same person as the original? Hick assumes it is reasonable to conceive of a place inhabited by resurrected persons, although this is entirely outside our experience

***examiner's* note** Hick broadly supports the biblical view, found in Revelation 21:1–2, that God will re-create humanity.

The ghost in the machine

Q1 What is a category error?

Q2 Explain the concept of the ghost in the machine.

Q3 How did Ryle illustrate the problems of a dualistic view of body and soul?

Q4 Identify one strength and one weakness of Ryle's argument.

ANSWERS

A1 to classify entities inappropriately, e.g. to categorise body and soul as separate, unrelated aspects of human nature

A2 the soul (the ghost) is an entity which drives the body (the machine); Ryle rejected the supposition that the origins of human behaviour must reside in an immaterial substance

A3 the foreigner who, having been shown the collegiate buildings in Oxford, asks 'Where's the university?'

A4 we are not consciously aware of body and soul as separate entities, but we do identify people by distinct bodily characteristics (e.g. red hair) or non-bodily characteristics (e.g. capacity for sympathy)

examiner's note Ryle also suggested another example of a category error: meeting uncle Joe, grandma and mum while wondering where the family really is.

Reincarnation

21 According to the Vedic tradition, what is the ultimate reality?

22 What do all souls seek?

23 What does 'atman' mean?

24 What is the purpose of reincarnation?

ANSWERS

the soul is re-clothed to live again in a new body

A1 Brahman or Brahma; Brahman is neutral and refers to the abstract, impersonal Absolute who is the cause of the universe; Brahma is masculine and a personal being; he is depicted as the first member of the Triad, who created the universe

A2 union with Brahman, achieved by understanding one's true self

A3 self; in the Upanishads it came to mean the true or inner self, the innermost nature of every living being

A4 the soul moves from life to life until it finds the ultimate truth; reincarnation also explains the differences between individuals

examiner's **note** Be ready to compare and contrast this approach with Western theories.

Near-death experiences

21 Identify three key features of a near-death experience.

22 What have critics said these near-death experiences could be?

23 What is cryptomnesia?

24 Identify three criteria for testing near-death experiences.

ANSWERS

A1 floating out of the body; travelling through a tunnel of light; meeting a religious figure or dead relative; feelings of peace; reaching a barrier and being turned back; life review; sudden return to the body

A2 hallucinations or delusions caused by reduced oxygen and increased carbon dioxide in the brain

A3 remembering a subconscious memory

A4 the explanation must be *coherent* and *specific*; a theory should not posit extra, or supernatural, realms without good reason; the theory should provide testable predictions

***examiner's* note** In writing examination answers on near-death experiences, don't confine yourself to statements of knowledge. You must go beyond the facts, and question the truth or otherwise of the statement.

 **75 ANSWERS**

Philosophical problems posed by life after death

21 What linguistic problems arise when speaking of life after death?

22 How might these linguistic problems be resolved?

23 Identify three reasons why people might reject a belief in the afterlife.

24 Identify three arguments which support belief in a post-mortem existence.

ANSWERS

the concept of life after death in itself may be considered to be logically flawed

A1 is it meaningful to speak of life after death, since life and death are mutually exclusive?; can personal pronouns be used to identify people in the afterlife, or do they belong exclusively to life in this world?

A2 by use of language games — talk of life after death is meaningful to those who are part of the language game, but not to those outside the game

A3 lack of verification; it is merely a comfort for those afraid of death; it is used as a device to keep people satisfied with their lot in this life

A4 we sense that there must be something beyond the physical life; the moral law needs to be balanced; it fulfils the promises of scripture

***examiner's* note** Never assume that the concepts of heaven and hell are not accepted as literally true by all religious believers.

Religious language (1)

Q1 What is cognitive language?

Q2 What is non-cognitive language?

Q3 What is meant by 'anti-realist'?

Q3 What is meant by 'realist'?

ANSWERS

language used to speak of God and features of religious belief and practice

A1 factual assertions about things which have objective or real existence

A2 non-factual assertions; language about matters which may be considered to be true, but not objectively real

A3 denying the objective reality of certain entities or insisting that we should be agnostic (uncertain) about their real existence

A4 the view that physical objects exist independently of our ability to perceive them; when I leave the room the table does not cease to exist

***examiner's* note** You need to be certain of the meaning of these key terms before you tackle religious language in further detail. They have to be applied to every theory within the topic.

Religious language (2)

21 Explain what is meant by the correspondence theory of truth.

22 Explain what is meant by the coherence theory of truth.

23 What is an analytic statement?

24 What is a synthetic statement?

ANSWERS

religious language is open to serious questioning as to whether it conveys factual information

A1 language claims which correspond to a given reality; for example, the statement 'the cat is brown' corresponds to the brown cat I can observe

A2 language claims which cohere to (fit in with) other, related beliefs; for example, the statement 'evil-doers will be punished in the afterlife' coheres to a set of beliefs about death, judgement, heaven and hell

A3 a statement which is confirmed true by definition, for example 'a circle is round' or 'if I am taller than you, you are shorter than me'

A4 an empirical proposition, verified or falsified through observation

***examiner's* note** Questions about religious language invariably ask you to consider the meaningfulness of claims. This is not the same as asking whether they are believable or not, but whether they can be submitted to rigorous linguistic analysis.

 **78** **ANSWERS**

Analogy

21 What is the 'via negative'?

22 What is univocal and equivocal language?

23 How does analogy solve the problem of religious language?

24 Identify two problems of analogical religious language.

ANSWERS

'proportional similarities which also acknowledge dissimilar features' (D. Burrell)

A1 speaking of God by denying or negating all claims about his nature and character in order to avoid misunderstanding of the terms used

A2 univocal: words are applied to God in exactly the same way as to other beings; equivocal: words are applied to God entirely differently from other beings or items

A3 terms used of God are related to, but not the same as, terms applied to other beings; God's goodness is the cause of goodness in things in the world and his goodness is proportional to God, not to humans

A4 analogies may anthropomorphise God; not all words can be applied to God analogically

examiner's **note** Ian Ramsey proposed models and qualifiers: the human attribute is the model which is qualified when applied to God, so it is infinitely enhanced.

 **ANSWERS**

The verification principle

Q1 With which philosophical school is the verification principle associated?

Q2 Outline the verification principle.

Q3 By what means could a statement be verified?

Q4 Distinguish between weak and strong verification.

ANSWERS ▶▶

a means of establishing the meaningfulness of language

A1 the Vienna Circle, later known as the Logical Positivists; A. J. Ayer's work *Language, Truth and Logic* was an influential exposition of the approach to language

A2 only statements which can be verified by observation or sense experience or which are analytically true can be said to be meaningful

A3 by empirical (synthetic) statements which could be tested; by mathematical statements; by tautologies

A4 weak verification allows meaning to statements which can be verified in principle; strong verification insists on direct verification

***examiner's* note** The strong verification principle effectively reduces all religious language claims to meaninglessness, since statements about God are neither analytically true nor open to empirical testing.

Criticisms of the verification principle

Q1 Why does the strong verification principle lead to absurd conclusions?

Q2 Why does the verification principle threaten the very kind of language which it attempted to support?

Q3 How could statements about God survive the challenge of the verification principle?

Q4 In what way is the verification principle intrinsically flawed?

 ANSWERS 〉〉

'this glittering new scalpel was, in one operation after the other, killing the patient' (B. McGee)

A1 too many types of language are rejected as meaningless, including historical statements, ethical statements and any personal opinions or feelings

A2 although it took a scientific approach to language, many scientific statements would fail the test, e.g. 'atoms exist'

A3 they may be eschatologically verified; God can verify claims about himself; religious experience can verify religious language claims

A4 it fails its own test; the principle is meaningless if the criteria are applied to it

examiner's **note** John Hick's parable of the celestial city provides an example of how religious language claims can be verified. It is also useful when writing about the problems of the religious ambiguity of the world and human experience.

The falsification principle

Q1 Which philosopher posed this principle as a challenge to the meaningfulness of religious language statements?

Q2 Explain the claim that religious language statements 'die the death of 1,000 qualifications'.

Q3 Give an example of circumstances in which a religious believer may qualify claims about God.

Q4 How did Basil Mitchell and R. M. Hare become involved in the falsification debate?

ANSWERS ▶▶

for a statement to be meaningful, it must be possible to say what would make it false

A1 Antony Flew

A2 in order to resolve problems about the nature of God or his failure to act in the world, statements about God are qualified rather than denied; Flew's challenge is that successive qualifications lead to a definition of God which is as good as no God at all

A3 God's failure to heal sickness, to deliver believers from difficult circumstances, to perform miracles, to be directly experienced

A4 Flew invited responses in the journal *University*; he drew particularly on those of Hare and Mitchell in his summing up

***examiner's* note** The falsification principle was initially developed by Karl Popper in the philosophy of science.

Responses to the falsification principle

Q1 What is a 'blik'?

Q2 Outline R. M. Hare's parable which illustrates the nature of a blik.

Q3 How does the notion of a blik save religious language statements from meaninglessness?

Q4 Why are bliks not confined to religious language claims?

ANSWERS

> '**to say something which may possibly be true, we must say something which may possibly be false**' (J. Hick)

A1 a way of regarding the world which is in principle neither verifiable nor falsifiable

A2 a lunatic believes all the dons want to murder him, and holds fast to this belief even when introduced to the friendliest dons; he allows nothing to count against his belief and everything potentially supports it

A3 bliks are meaningful to people who hold them since they make a difference to the way they live their lives

A4 we have bliks about things we take as a matter of trust — the lift we are in will not break down, or the plane we travel on will not crash

examiner's **note** Don't get bogged down in the parables. Learn brief versions and focus on evaluation.

(**83**) **ANSWERS**

The parable of the partisan and the stranger

Q1 Outline the parable of the partisan and the stranger.

Q2 What kind of faith does this parable support?

Q3 What three options does Mitchell identify as being open to the religious believer when making religious language claims?

Q4 Suggest a counter-argument to Mitchell's claims.

ANSWERS ▶▶

the parable distinguishes between recognising challenges to faith and allowing them to negate it

A1 a partisan meets a stranger who claims to be the leader of the resistance and urges the partisan to have faith in him; when the stranger appears to be withholding help, the partisan still believes that the stranger is on his side, because their original encounter has given him sufficient confidence to do so

A2 non-propositional faith based on some personal knowledge of God

A3 provisional hypotheses, easily discarded; vacuous formulae to which experience makes no difference; significant articles of faith

A4 as a human being, the partisan cannot always act as he would choose; God is not limited in the same way; the analogy therefore fails

examiner's **note** Basil Mitchell argues that religious beliefs, which are cognitive assertions, are falsifiable in principle but not in practice.

Language games

Q1 Which twentieth-century philosopher is associated with language game theory?

Q2 Explain the statement: 'Whereof one cannot speak, thereof one must be silent.'

Q3 What does Wittgenstein mean by 'form of life'?

Q4 Why is the *use* of language important to language game theory?

ANSWERS

a response to the potentially devastating consequences of verification

A1 Ludwig Wittgenstein

A2 Wittgenstein was alluding to the principle of verification, which made it impossible to speak meaningfully of anything which could not be verified

A3 the activity with which language is associated

A4 the use of language is determined by its context or 'form of life'; language can be used correctly or incorrectly — for example, in religious language, to describe God as 'scholarly' would not be an appropriate use of the term, whereas to describe him as 'benevolent' would be

***examiner's* note** Language game theory is associated with anti-realist language, since it does not demand that language should correspond to objective realities, but to cohere with an appropriate set of beliefs.

(85) ANSWERS

Symbol (1)

21 Identify three different types of symbol within religious language.

22 Which scholar described a symbol as participating in that which it conveyed?

23 What non-religious example of a symbol did he use to explain this?

24 Why may symbols be essential in religious language?

ANSWERS

non-literal forms of verbal, pictorial or demonstrative language

A1 the cross, a dove, a font, sacraments, religious vestments, certain foods; descriptive statements about the divine (e.g. 'God is a rock'); festivals; faith claims about Jesus (e.g. 'Jesus is alive today') or other religious leaders (e.g. 'Mohammed is the seal of the prophets')

A2 Paul Tillich

A3 a flag — it expresses feelings of patriotism and national identity as well as providing a convenient point of reference for practical purposes

A4 they are needed to convey essential truths of religion which are beyond everyday verbal communication

***examiner's* note** This is another anti-realist approach to religious language, which does not depend on claims having objective truth value. Hence, even faith claims could be understood symbolically.

Symbol (2)

21 How might symbols be conveyed in religious language?

22 What information might the symbol of the cross convey to a Christian?

23 In what ways might this information be lost in the modern use of the symbol?

24 How might symbols undermine the message they are intended to convey?

ANSWERS

A1 through narrative forms such as myths and allegories

A2 the sacrifice of Jesus, the need for salvation, hope of the resurrection, the love of God

A3 symbols become trivialised and overused: the use of the cross as jewellery does not always convey its religious meaning

A4 they become the focus of worship rather than helping the worshipper towards a greater understanding of what they represent

***examiner's* note** Rowan Williams observes: 'Like all other serious human discourse, religious language requires a symbolic foundation.'

87 ANSWERS

Myth (1)

21 Identify the way myth is used in religious language.

22 Identify two examples of religious myth.

23 What is demythologisation?

24 Identify two problems of mythological language.

ANSWERS

'myth is a symbolic, approximate expression of truth' (Millar Burrows)

A1 to convey non-historical, supernatural beliefs, frequently using symbols within a narrative structure

A2 the creation narratives; the birth narratives of Jesus; the Resurrection; miracles; eschatological teaching

A3 the process of stripping the mythological elements from a religious text, leaving the core of the religious message

A4 it is not easy to separate literal and non-literal teachings; believing that the events conveyed by myth actually happened is important for many believers

***examiner's* note** Rudolph Bultmann claimed: 'It is impossible to use electric light and the wireless and to avail ourselves of modern medical and surgical discoveries and at the same time to believe in the New Testament world of demons and spirits.'

Myth (2)

21 What literary forms may be used in myth?

22 What is an aetiological myth?

23 What is apocalyptic myth?

24 How did D. F. Strauss redefine the use of myth?

ANSWERS 》

an anti-realist form of non-cognitive language

A1 symbols, metaphors, similes, narratives, parables, allegories

A2 a mythological form which attempts to explain how things came to be

A3 a mythological form which deals with the future revelation of hidden truths

A4 he suggested that the focus of myths should be the story which contains the mythological symbols, rather than that mythology itself

***examiner's* note** J. W. Rogerson observes: '[Myths are]…of value to traditions that seek to describe the action of the other worldly in the present world.'

God and morality

Critically analyse the claim: 'Morality proves the existence of God.'

ANSWERS

the key words are 'critically analyse'

This claim revolves around the view that God provides standards of good and bad, and right and wrong. Therefore, in order to be moral beings, humans must obey God and, consequently, morality proves God exists.

However, this is not the whole picture. While it may be true that religious belief may be linked to moral behaviour, being good does not prove that God is there. We may act in a certain way because of our upbringing, background, culture or other reasons. Morality does not prove the existence of God — why, otherwise, do non-religious people often behave as well as religious believers?

examiner's **note** Be careful to read examination questions like these properly — don't concentrate too much on the facts, but look to criticise the premise. Ask yourself 'How far is this right and how far is it wrong? What are the alternatives?' Remember, a question will never ask you to be critical if there is nothing to be critical about.

The Cosmological Argument

To what extent does the Cosmological Argument offer convincing proof of the existence of God?

ANSWERS

weigh up whether the argument gives proof of God's existence or merely offers God as an explanation

From our understanding of the laws of nature and the universe, it seems that everything is dependent on other things or actions. Since nothing can come out of nothing, this would suggest, logically, that the first cause was not, itself, caused or dependent upon anything else. Therefore, if God is the first cause, God exists.

However, it is not an entirely satisfactory explanation, since we do not know all the laws of nature and there may be other events or causes that we know nothing about. It is, therefore, a strong and persuasive argument, but not a totally convincing one.

examiner's **note** Don't fall into the trap of saying that any one particular argument is totally convincing proof of the existence of God. The wisest approach is to ensure that you know the strengths and weaknesses of all the arguments and to evaluate accordingly — but always leave room for doubt. In philosophy, nothing is absolutely certain.

 **(91) ANSWERS**

The Design Argument

To what extent is the Design Argument a convincing proof of the existence of God?

ANSWERS

The strengths of the Design Argument are considerable: it has a biblical basis, uses empirical evidence and accords with many scientific principles. It is a particularly convincing argument for religious believers since it supports many traditional beliefs about God in an apparently philosophical way.

However, criticisms of it are equally formidable: the creator need not be God and we do not know enough about the nature of the universe to make truth claims about the creator.

Therefore, it is not a totally convincing proof of the existence of God; it offers one explanation, but there are many others which may be equally, or more, convincing.

***examiner's* note** In this question, be open-minded and offer and evaluate the reasons on both sides — don't just weigh in on one side and ignore the other. If you do, you risk losing marks for not evaluating all the evidence properly.

The Ontological Argument

How far does the Ontological Argument succeed as a proof for the existence of God?

ANSWERS

The argument could be said to offer strong grounds for proof if its premises are universally agreed to be analytically true. If so, then the conclusion cannot be false and the argument must prove by flawless logic that God exists. Furthermore, the argument cannot be hindered by empirical claims that are based on inaccurate and subjective empirical evidence or observation. The argument confirms and clarifies what the believer holds to be true and, as such, may be considered valuable in supporting a classical theistic view of God.

However, the premises cannot be assumed to be true. The claim that God is that than which nothing greater can be conceived is a tenet of faith, and is not necessarily objectively true. To say that God is supremely perfect and cannot not exist is an assumption of classical theism. The Ontological Argument does not rely on probability, but to be successful it must rest on an unchallengeable first premise.

***examiner's* note** Although Aquinas believed that God's existence was self-evident, he acknowledged that not everyone has the same idea of God.

(93) ANSWERS

The argument from religious experience

If experience of God proves his existence, does the lack of experience of God prove he does not exist?

ANSWERS

This view is supported by Michael Martin who proposes a negative principle of credulity: 'If it seems to a subject S that X is absent, then probably X is absent.' However, Richard Swinburne argues that we cannot experience the absence of God because we do not know how God would be experienced if he existed. Arguably, this also means that we could not know if we had experienced God if he did appear.

The absence of God for some need not prove he does not exist, or cancel out others' experiences of him. Brian Davies uses the example of two groups of explorers in the jungle. One sees the animal they are hunting, the other does not, but the lack of experience of the second group does not discount the experience of the first.

***examiner's* note** Consider whether, if a person's life is changed for the better after an illusory religious experience, that experience was more or less valid than a genuine religious experience which had no impact on the experient's life.

Moral and theological problems of miracles

How far can miracles be criticised on moral and theological grounds?

ANSWERS

the arbitrariness of miracles makes them susceptible to criticism

According to scripture, God is all-loving, powerful and just. However, in terms of miracles, God does not appear to treat his creation equally or justly; miracles happen for some people and not for others, in a random and unfathomable fashion. Peter Vardy cites the example of God miraculously healing an old man at Lourdes while failing to help starving millions in Ethiopia. Other scholars, such as Maurice Wiles, highlight the testimonies of apparently trivial miracles, yet question God's failure to act against the horrors of the Second World War. Moreover, the scriptures urge humans to behave towards each other with love and kindness, yet God seems to be prepared to watch people suffer and not come to their aid.

However, this is not altogether fair. Jesus Christ did not heal every sick person he met (see John 5) and performed his miracles purely as a sign of God's power, in order to help people to believe in his saving message. It could be argued that the purpose of miracles is not to make everything all right, but to increase people's faith in God.

examiner's **note** It needs only one of the millions of testimonies about miracles to be shown to be true for the existence of God to be proved.

95 **ANSWERS**

The problem of evil

To what extent is the problem of evil an insurmountable one for religious believers?

ANSWERS ▶▶

The problem of evil may be thought to be insurmountable because all attempts to resolve it can be challenged, invariably by the claim that theodicies are no more than qualifications of the nature of God. Irrespective of the reason why God may refrain from acting in the face of evil, he withholds his power or his love — hence the believer has to admit that 'God is loving/powerful, but …' Furthermore, religious believers may be guilty of allowing nothing to count against the existence and the nature of God.

Theodicies fail to address the real issue of the problem and offer unconvincing reasons as to why God permits evil and suffering. Hence, while believers may be convinced that they have solved the problem, it will be difficult to persuade atheists that the solution is acceptable. However, for believers, solving the problem is a personal matter, and if they have found a solution which satisfies them, they may be unconcerned as to whether the atheist is also satisfied.

***examiner's* note** The key to this question is the observation that no theodicy is entirely fail-safe, but since religious belief is so personal, atheists are on no stronger ground than theists.

96 ANSWERS

Reconciling scientific and religious interpretations of the origin of the world

To what extent may religious and scientific interpretations of the origin of the world be reconciled with each other?

ANSWERS

the key phrase is 'to what extent': present arguments for and against the case and draw a conclusion

The division between science and religion is relatively recent; it rests on the assumption that religious explanations of the universe are based on unsound data which treat mythological or metaphorical texts as factually true. Similarly, scientific explanations for the origin of the universe are viewed as offering verifiable, factual data, overturning all faith-based interpretations.

If both approaches are assumed to be asking the same questions, they are incompatible. However, while Peter Akins argues: 'We can even begin to discern how the universe could come from absolute nothing', Keith Ward observes: 'Science is based on the postulate that one should always seek reasons for why things are as they are … If I ask "Why does water boil as it is heated?" I do not expect to be told, "There is no reason at all. It just does."' Ward suggests that asking questions about the universe is appropriate to both religion and science, and both are able to offer useful answers to those questions.

***examiner's* note** There are many ways of approaching this question and many scholars you can refer to. Ensure that you offer a balanced argument.

 **97) ANSWERS**

Atheism

Critically evaluate the claim that the existence of God cannot be disproved.

ANSWERS

If it is not possible to prove decisively the existence of God, it must also be impossible to disprove it. It is questionable whether the atheist really is on any stronger ground than the theist, bearing in mind that the same rules of proof and probability must apply to an atheistic argument as to a theistic one. The biblical writers did not countenance the possibility of atheism or suggest that it may have any intellectual or philosophical credibility: it is 'the fool' who has 'said in his heart there is no God' (Psalm 10:4; 53:1). However, theists may argue that even within theistic belief there remains an element of agnosticism, since the transcendent God is ultimately unknowable and cannot be assumed to be known fully. Nevertheless, Francis Collins observes: 'Of all choices, atheism requires the greatest faith, as it demands that one's limited store of human knowledge is sufficient to exclude the possibility of God.'

***examiner's* note** A question of this type requires you to have an understanding of the nature of philosophical proof. Make sure you know this material very well.

Life after death

To what extent is a belief in life after death philosophically valid?

ANSWERS

the key terms here are 'philosophically valid'

To be philosophically valid, belief in life after death must be coherent, meaningful and free from flaws of logic and reasoning. Problems posed by a belief in life after death include: lack of verification; linguistic problems; the fact that it is a faith-based belief; problems of establishing where personal identity lies; the difficulties of conceiving a post-mortem existence so far removed from earthly existence; reconciling different perspectives on the afterlife.

However, we could challenge the view that belief in life after death has to fulfil any criteria of meaningfulness, since it is part of religious faith which is, by its very nature, unverifiable. Belief in life after death is subject only to eschatological verification, which makes it verifiable in principle and hence meaningful. Talk of life after death can also be understood when used correctly within the appropriate language game, i.e. only through knowledge of the context in which a statement is made can we fully understand it.

examiner's note Bear in mind that this question does not ask you to give factual detail of different possible forms of the afterlife. You could critique these here, but only if you identify their philosophical problems.

Religious language

Assess the view that religious language is meaningless.

ANSWERS

Religious language statements may be considered meaningless if it is assumed that they must be open to formal, logical or empirical verification. Since claims about the invisible God or about events in the past ('Jesus rose from the dead') or the future ('there will be a last judgement') are not strictly verifiable, they may be dismissed as having no value. The falsification principle identifies the problem of failing to allow anything to count against religious language claims and rendering them meaningless by qualification.

Symbolic and mythological language cannot be verified or falsified, since they are essentially anti-realist forms of language which must be used in their right context or fail to have meaning. However, if religious language is understood to operate within the religious language game, its meaning is grasped by those who use it and it coheres with the beliefs and ideas appropriate to that game or 'form of life'. Religious language statements could also be eschatologically verifiable, thus giving them meaning.

examiner's **note** You may be asked this kind of question in relation to one or more types of religious language, so be prepared to be flexible. It is an open-ended question.

(100) ANSWERS